THE FALSE GODS
WE WORSHIP

and

THE ABUNDANT LIFE

THE FALSE GODS WE WORSHIP

and

THE ABUNDANT LIFE

Spencer W. Kimball

CLASSIC TALK SERIES

Deseret Book Company
Salt Lake City, Utah

Reprinted with permission.

Library of Congress Catalog Card Number: 97-78186

ISBN 0-87579-882-9

Printed in the United States of America   72082-4585E

10   9   8   7   6   5   4   3

THE FALSE GODS
WE WORSHIP

I have heard that the sense most closely associated with memory is the sense of smell. If this is true, then perhaps it explains the many pleasing feelings that overtake me these mornings when I am able to step outdoors for a few moments and breathe in the warm and comfortable aromas that I have come to associate over the years with the soil and vegetation of this good earth.

Now and then, when the moment is right, some particular scent—perhaps only the green grass, or the smell of sage brought from a distance by a breeze—will take me back to the days of my youth in Arizona. It was an arid country, yet it was fruitful under the hands of determined laborers.

We worked with the land and the cattle in all kinds of weather, and when we traveled it was on horseback or in open wagons or carriages, mostly. I used to run like the wind with my brothers and sisters through the orchards, down the dusty lanes, past rows of corn, red tomatoes, onions, squash. Because of this, I suppose it is natural to think that in those days we were closer to elemental life.

Some time ago I chanced to walk outdoors when the dark and massive clouds of an early afternoon thunderstorm were gathering; and as the large raindrops began to drum the dusty soil with increasing rapidity, I recalled the occasional summer afternoons when I was a boy when the tremendous thunderheads would gather over the hills and bring welcome rain to the thirsty soil of the valley floor. We children would run for the shed, and while the lightning danced about we would sit and watch, transfixed, marveling at the ever-increasing power of the pounding rainfall. Afterward, the air would be clean and cool and filled with the sweet smells of the soil, the trees, and the plants of the garden.

There were evenings those many years ago, at about sunset, when I would walk in with the cows. Stopping by a tired old fence post, I would sometimes just stand silently in the mellow light and the fragrance of sunflowers and ask myself, "If you were going to create a world, what would it be like?" Now with a little thought the answer seems so natural: "Just like this one."

So on this day while I stood watching the thunderstorm, I felt—and I feel now—that this is a marvelous earth on which we find ourselves: and when I thought of our preparations for the United States Bicentennial celebration I felt a deep gratitude to the Lord for the choice land and the people and institutions of America. There is much that is good in this land, and much to love.

Nevertheless, on this occasion of so many pleasant memories another impression assailed my thoughts. The dark and threatening clouds that hung so low over the valley seemed to force my mind back to a theme that the Brethren have concerned themselves with for many years now—indeed a theme that has often occupied the attention of the Lord's chosen prophets since the world began. I am speaking of the general state of wickedness in which we seem to find the world in these perilous yet crucially momentous days; and thinking of this, I am reminded of the general principle that where much is given, much is expected (see Luke 12:48).

The Lord gave us a choice world and expects righteousness and obedience to his commandments in return. But when I review the performance of this people in comparison with what is expected, I am appalled and frightened. Iniquity seems to abound. The Destroyer seems to be taking full advantage of the time remaining to him in this, the great day of his power. Evil seems about to engulf us like a great wave, and we feel that truly we are living in conditions similar to those in the days of Noah before the Flood.

I have traveled much in various assignments over the years, and when I pass through the lovely countryside or fly over the vast and beautiful expanses of our globe, I compare these beauties with many of the dark and miserable practices of men, and I have the feeling that the good earth can hardly bear our presence upon it. I recall the occasion when Enoch heard the earth mourn, saying, "Wo, wo is me, the mother of men; I am pained, I am weary, because of the wickedness of my children. When shall I rest, and be cleansed from the filthiness which is gone forth out of me?" (Moses 7:48).

The Brethren constantly cry out against that which is intolerable in the sight of the Lord: against pollution of mind, body, and our surroundings; against vulgarity, stealing, lying, pride, and blasphemy; against fornication, adultery, homosexuality, and all other abuses of the sacred power to create; against murder and all that is like unto it; against all manner of desecration.

That such a cry should be necessary among a people so blessed is amazing to me. And that such things should be found even among the Saints to some degree is scarcely believable, for these are a people who are in possession of many gifts of the Spirit, who have knowledge that puts the eternities into perspective, who have been shown the way to eternal life.

Sadly, however, we find that to be shown the way is not necessarily to walk in it, and many have not been able to continue in faith. These have submitted themselves in one degree or another to the enticings of Satan and his servants and joined with those of "the world" in lives of ever-deepening idolatry.

I use the word *idolatry* intentionally. As I study ancient scripture, I am more and more convinced that there is significance in the fact that the commandment "Thou shalt have no other gods before me" is the first of the Ten Commandments.

Few men have ever knowingly and deliberately chosen to reject God and his blessings. Rather, we learn from the scriptures that because the exercise of faith has always appeared to be more difficult than relying on things more immediately at hand, carnal man has tended to transfer his trust from God to material things. Therefore, in all ages when men have fallen under the power of Satan and lost the faith, they have put in its place a hope in the "arm of flesh" and in "gods of silver, and gold, of brass, iron, wood, and stone, which see not, nor hear, nor know" (Daniel 5:23)—that is, in idols. This I find to be a dominant theme in the Old Testament. Whatever thing a man sets his heart and his trust in most is his god; and if his god doesn't also happen to be the true and living God of Israel, that man is laboring in idolatry.

It is my firm belief that when we read these scriptures and try to "liken them unto [our]-selves," as Nephi suggested (1 Nephi 19:24), we will see many parallels between the ancient worship of graven images and behavioral patterns in our very own experience.

The Lord has blessed us as a people with

a prosperity unequaled in times past. The resources that have been placed in our power are good, and necessary to our work here on the earth. But I am afraid that many of us have been surfeited with flocks and herds and acres and barns and wealth and have begun to worship them as false gods, and they have power over us. Do we have more of these good things than our faith can stand? Many people spend most of their time working in the service of a self-image that includes sufficient money, stocks, bonds, investment portfolios, property, credit cards, furnishings, automobiles, and the like to *guarantee* carnal security throughout, it is hoped, a long and happy life. Forgotten is the fact that our assignment is to use these many resources in our families and quorums to build up the kingdom of God—to further the missionary effort and the genealogical and temple work; to raise our children up as fruitful servants unto the Lord; to bless others in every way, that they may also be fruitful. Instead, we expend these blessings on our own desires, and as Moroni said, "Ye adorn yourselves with that which hath no life, and yet suffer the hungry, and the needy, and the naked, and the sick and the afflicted to pass by you, and notice them not" (Mormon 8:39).

As the Lord himself said in our day, "They seek not the Lord to establish his righteousness, but every man walketh in his own way, and after the image of his own god, whose image is in the likeness of the world, and *whose substance is that of an idol*, which waxeth old and shall perish in Babylon, even Babylon the great, which shall fall" (D&C 1:16; emphasis added).

One man I know of was called to a position of service in the Church, but he felt that he couldn't accept because his investments required more attention and more of his time than he could spare for the Lord's work. He left the service of the Lord in search of Mammon, and he is a millionaire today.

But I recently learned an interesting fact: If a man owns a million dollars worth of gold at today's prices, he possesses approximately one 27-billionth of all the gold that is present in the earth's thin crust alone. This is an amount so small in proportion as to be inconceivable to the mind of man. But there is more to this: The Lord who created and has power over all the earth created many other earths as well, even "worlds without number" (Moses 1:33); and when this man received the oath and covenant of the priesthood (D&C 84:33–44), he received a promise from the Lord of "all that my Father hath" (v. 38). To set aside all these great promises in favor of a chest of gold and a sense of carnal security is a mistake in perspective of colossal proportions. To think that he has settled for so little is a saddening and pitiful prospect indeed; the souls of men are far more precious than this.

One young man, when called on a mission, replied that he didn't have much talent for that kind of thing. What he was good at was keeping his powerful new automobile in top condition. He enjoyed the sense of power and acceleration, and when he was driving, the continual motion gave him the illusion that he was really getting somewhere.

All along, his father had been content with saying, "He likes to do things with his hands. That's good enough for him."

Good enough for a son of God? This young man didn't realize that the power of his automobile is infinitesimally small in comparison with the power of the sea, or of the sun; and there are many suns, all controlled by law and by priesthood, ultimately—a priesthood power that he could have been developing in the service of the

Lord. He settled for a pitiful god, a composite of steel and rubber and shiny chrome.

An older couple retired from the world of work and also, in effect, from the Church. They purchased a pickup truck and camper and, separating themselves from all obligations, set out to see the world and simply enjoy what little they had accumulated the rest of their days. They had no time for the temple, were too busy for genealogical research and for missionary service. He lost contact with his high priests quorum and was not home enough to work on his personal history. Their experience and leadership were sorely needed in their branch, but, unable to "endure to the end," they were not available.

I am reminded of an article I read some years ago about a group of men who had gone to the jungles to capture monkeys. They tried a number of different things to catch the monkeys, including nets. But finding that the nets could injure such small creatures, they finally came upon an ingenious solution. They built a large number of small boxes, and in the top of each they bored a hole just large enough for a monkey to get his hand into. They then set these boxes out under the trees and in each one they put a nut that the monkeys were particularly fond of.

When the men left, the monkeys began to come down from the trees and examine the boxes. Finding that there were nuts to be had, they reached into the boxes to get them. But when a monkey would try to withdraw his hand with the nut, he could not get his hand out of the box because his little fist, with the nut inside, was now too large.

At about this time, the men would come out of the underbrush and converge on the monkeys. And here is the curious thing: When the monkeys saw the men coming, they would shriek and scramble about with the thought of escaping; but as easy as it would have been, they would not let go of the nut so that they could withdraw their hands from the boxes and thus escape. The men captured them easily.

And so it often seems to be with people. They have such a firm grasp on things of the world—that which is telestial—that no amount of urging and no degree of emergency can persuade them to let go in favor of that which is celestial. Satan gets them in his grip easily. If we insist on spending all our time and resources building up for ourselves a worldly kingdom, that is exactly what we will inherit.

In spite of our delight in defining ourselves as modern, and our tendency to think we possess a sophistication that no people in the past ever had—in spite of these things, we are, on the whole, an idolatrous people—a condition most repugnant to the Lord.

We are a warlike people, easily distracted from our assignment of preparing for the coming of the Lord. When enemies rise up, we commit vast resources to the fabrication of gods of stone and steel—ships, planes, missiles, fortifications—and depend on them for protection and deliverance. When threatened, we become antienemy instead of pro-kingdom of God; we train a man in the art of war and call him a patriot, thus, in the manner of Satan's counterfeit of true patriotism, perverting the Savior's teaching:

"Love your enemies, bless them that curse you, do good to them that hate you, and pray for them which despitefully use you, and persecute you;

"That ye may be the children of your Father which is in heaven" (Matthew 5:44–45).

We forget that if we are righteous the Lord will either not suffer our enemies to come upon us—and this is the special promise to the inhabitants of the land of the Americas (see 2 Nephi 1:7)—or he will fight our battles for us (see Exodus 14:14; D&C 98:37, to name only two references of many). This he is able to do, for as he said at the time of his betrayal, "Thinkest thou that I cannot now pray to my Father, and he shall presently give me more than twelve legions of angels?" (Matthew 26:53). We can imagine what fearsome soldiers they would be. King Jehoshaphat and his people were delivered by such a troop (see 2 Chronicles 20), and when Elisha's life was threatened, he comforted his servant by saying, "Fear not: for they that be with us are more than they that be with them" (2 Kings 6:16). The Lord then opened the eyes of the servant, "And he saw: and, behold, the mountain was full of horses and chariots of fire round about Elisha" (v. 17).

Enoch, too, was a man of great faith who

would not be distracted from his duties by the enemy: "And so great was the faith of Enoch that he led the people of God, and their enemies came to battle against them; and he spake the word of the Lord, and the earth trembled, and the mountains fled, even according to his command; and the rivers of water were turned out of their course; and the roar of the lions was heard out of the wilderness; and all nations feared greatly, so powerful was the word of Enoch" (Moses 7:13).

What are we to fear when the Lord is with us? Can we not take the Lord at his word and exercise a particle of faith in him? Our assignment is affirmative: to forsake the things of the world as ends in themselves; to leave off idolatry and press forward in faith; to carry the gospel to our enemies, that they might no longer be our enemies.

We must leave off the worship of modern-day idols and a reliance on the "arm of flesh," for the

Lord has said to all the world in our day, "I will not spare any that remain in Babylon" (D&C 64:24).

When Peter preached such a message as this to the people on the day of Pentecost, many of them "were pricked in their heart, and said unto Peter and to the rest of the apostles, Men and brethren, what shall we do?" (Acts 2:37).

And Peter answered: "Repent, and be baptized every one of you in the name of Jesus Christ for the remission of sins, and . . . receive the gift of the Holy Ghost" (v. 38).

As we near the year 2,000, our message is the same as that which Peter gave. And further, that which the Lord himself gave "unto the ends of the earth, that all that will hear may hear:

"Prepare ye, prepare ye for that which is to come, for the Lord is nigh" (D&C 1:11–12).

We believe that the way for each person and each family to prepare as the Lord has directed is to begin to exercise greater faith, to repent, and to enter into the work of his kingdom on earth, which is The Church of Jesus Christ of Latter-day Saints. It may seem a little difficult at first, but when a person begins to catch a vision of the true work, when he begins to see something of eternity in its true perspective, the blessings begin to far outweigh the cost of leaving "the world" behind.

Herein lies the only true happiness, and therefore we invite and welcome all men, everywhere, to join in this work. For those who are determined to serve the Lord at all costs, this is the way to eternal life. All else is but a means to that end.

From a First Presidency message, "The False Gods We Worship," published while President Kimball was serving as president of The Church of Jesus Christ of Latter-day Saints (see *Ensign*, June 1976, 3–6).

THE ABUNDANT LIFE

J esus of Nazareth observed in his teachings the following:

"I am come that they might have life, and that they might have it more abundantly" (John 10:10).

This statement is sometimes misconstrued to mean that his teachings pertain only to ways in which mortality, or this life, can be a richer and deeper experience.

On the other hand, there was a time in religious history when people made the mistake of thinking that Christianity belonged only to

another world yet to come. That idea led some
to take a negative rather than a positive view of
this life; it also dampened efforts to improve the
human condition.

Today, more often than not, a balance needs to
be struck by reminding ourselves that true
Christianity is not something that is only mortal
in its implications. Applying the teachings of
Jesus Christ here and now can make this life
richer and more abundant, but ultimately true
Christianity focuses on man's opportunity to tri-
umph over all his enemies, including death.

Jesus of Nazareth came into the world to
bring to pass the Atonement, which gives to all
men everywhere immortality through the gift of
Resurrection. Thus Jesus' teachings can clearly
help us to live a righteous life and to be happier
here, but his great sacrifice guarantees to us
immortality and the extension of our individual
identity and life beyond the grave. Of course,

there are those who do not accept the reality of the resurrection—and that is their privilege and their loss—but it is impossible to speak of the abundant life without speaking of life as a continuum. This life, this narrow sphere we call mortality, does not, within the short space of time we are allowed here, give to all of us perfect justice, perfect health, or perfect opportunities. Perfect justice, however, will come eventually through a divine plan, as will the perfection of all other conditions and blessings—to those who have lived to merit them.

It is appropriate to note the ways in which the teachings of Jesus of Nazareth can be crucial in the living of our daily lives in this tiny sliver of time that we call mortality.

First, service to others deepens and sweetens this life while we are preparing to live in a better world. It is by serving that we learn how to serve. When we are engaged in the service of our fellowmen, not only do our deeds assist them, but we put our own problems in a fresher perspective. When we concern ourselves more with others, there is less time to be concerned with ourselves! In the midst of the miracle of serving, there is the promise of Jesus that by losing ourselves, we find ourselves!

Not only do we "find" ourselves in terms of acknowledging divine guidance in our lives, but the more we serve our fellowmen in appropriate ways, the more substance there is to our souls. We become more significant individuals as we serve others. We become more substantive as we serve others—indeed, it is easier to "find" ourselves because there is so much more of us to find!

George McDonald observed that "it is by loving and not by being loved that one can come nearest to the soul of another." Of course, we all need to be loved, but we must be giving and not

always receiving, if we want to have the wholeness of our lives and a reinforced sense of
purpose.

Second, Jesus' teachings help us to have a cor-
rect view of life and our circumstances. Sometimes the solution is not to change our circumstance, but to change our attitude about that
circumstance and its difficulties so that we see
more clearly our opportunities for more abundant service. It has been said that hell is to be
frozen in self-pity.

Someone else observed:

"If we are not careful, we can be injured by
the frostbite of frustration; we can be frozen in
place by the chill of unmet expectations. To
avoid this we must—just as we would with arc-
tic coldness—keep moving, keep serving, and
keep reaching out, so that our own immobility
does not become our chief danger."

God does notice us, and he watches over us.

But it is usually through another person that he meets our needs. Therefore, it is vital that we serve each other. The abundant life is also achieved as we magnify our view of life, expand our view of others *and* our own possibilities. Thus the more we follow the teachings of the Master, the more enlarged our perspective becomes. We see many more possibilities for service than we would have seen without this magnification. There is great security in spirituality, and we cannot have spirituality without service!

The abundant life, of course, has little to do with the acquisition of material things, though there are many wonderful individuals who have been blessed materially and who use their wealth to help their fellowmen—and this is most commendable. The abundant life noted in the scriptures is the spiritual sum that is arrived at by the multiplying of our service to others and by investing our talents in service to God and to man. Jesus said, you will recall, that on the first two commandments hang all the law and the prophets, and those two command- ments involve developing our love of God, of self, of our neighbors, and of all men. There can be no real abundance in life that is not connected with the keeping and the carrying out of those two great commandments.

Unless the way we live draws us closer to our Heavenly Father and to our fellowmen, there will be an enormous emptiness in our lives. It is frightening for me to see, for instance, how the lifestyle of so many today causes them to disen- gage from their families and their friends and their peers toward a heedless pursuit of pleasure or materialism. So often loyalty to family, to com- munity, and to country is pushed aside in favor of other pursuits which are wrongly thought to be productive of happiness when, in fact, selfishness is so often the pursuit of questionable pleasure which passes so quickly. One of the differences between true joy and mere pleasure is that certain pleasures are realized only at the cost of someone else's pain. Joy, on the other hand, springs out of selflessness and service, and it benefits rather than hurts others.

Some observers might wonder why we concern ourselves with such simple things as service to others in a world surrounded by such dramatic problems. Yet, one of the advantages of the gospel of Jesus Christ is that it gives us perspective about the people on this planet, including ourselves, so that we can see the things that truly matter and avoid getting caught up in the multiplicity of lesser causes that vie for the attention of mankind.

If we would truly reform mankind, we must first reform ourselves. It was a wise man who observed with regard to improvement that so

often everyone meddles in everyone else's mat-
ters instead of improving himself—and thus
everything stays the same. The abundant life
begins from within and then moves outward to
other individuals. If there is richness and righteousness in us, then we can make a difference
in the lives of others, just as key individuals
have influenced the lives of each of us for good
and made us richer than we otherwise would
have been.

If you and I would be good leaders, we
should reflect periodically on the qualities of
those who have served, led, and taught us.
Select just two or three individuals in your life
who have been most influential, and ask yourself what they did specifically that was most
helpful to you at the critical, important times of
your life. On reflecting for a few moments, you
are apt to conclude that such people really cared
for you, that they took time out for you, that

they taught you something you needed to know. Reflect now upon your performance—as I do on mine—as to whether or not we embody in our lives those same basic helpful attributes.

It is less likely, in stirring through one's memories, that someone will be remembered because that individual used particularly influential techniques. Most often someone has served and helped us by giving us love and understanding, by taking time to assist us, by showing us the way through the light of his or her own example. I cannot stress enough, therefore, the importance of your doing these same things for those who will now depend upon you, just as you have depended upon others to serve you in the past by special leadership and special teaching.

If you were to think and to reflect and to identify those individuals who have been most influential in your life, this would give you perspective and would help you on your way to happiness. Upon reflection, you will no doubt find that these are individuals who have, in one way or another, achieved much by way of living the abundant life. Remember that true love is never wasted and true service is never without some significance.

I cannot be true to my task or my calling in speaking of "The Abundant Life" without noting also that the same Jesus who spoke of having life more abundantly gave us some ground rules in his gospel which will produce that abundance in life and that happiness about which he spoke. There are many causes for human suffering—including war, disease, and poverty—and the suffering that proceeds from each of these is very real, but I would not be true to my trust if I did not say that the most persistent cause of human suffering, that suffering which causes the deepest pain, is sin—the violation of the commandments given to us by God.

There cannot be, for instance, a rich and full life unless we practice total chastity before marriage and total fidelity after. There cannot be a sense of wholeness and integrity if we lie, steal, or cheat. There cannot be sweetness in our lives if we are filled with envy or covetousness. Our lives cannot really be abundant if we do not honor our parents. If any of us wish to have more precise prescriptions for ourselves in terms of what we can do to have more abundant lives, all we usually need to do is to consult our conscience.

May I counsel you that when you select causes for which you give your time and talents and treasure in service to others, be careful to select good causes. There are so many of these causes to which you can give yourself fully and freely and which will produce much joy and happiness for you and for those you serve. There are other causes, from time to time, which

may seem more fashionable and which may produce the applause of the world, but these are
usually more selfish in nature. These latter
causes tend to arise out of what the scriptures
call "the commandments of men" rather than
the commandments of God. Such causes have
some virtues and some usefulness, but they are
not as important as those causes which grow out
of keeping the commandments of God.

You will find that the more you reflect upon
what must be done to have a richer and more
abundant life, the more you will be led back to
central considerations that are contained in the
messages of the Master. If we follow in his foot-
steps, we can live by faith rather than by fear. If
we can share his perspective about people, we
can love them, serve them, and reach out to
them—rather than feeling anxious and threatened by others.

During youth and young maturity, time flies

with great speed. To travel listlessly is just futile. One should have a destination and a goal to reach. One should determine what he wants out of life and then bend every effort toward reaching that goal. He must realize that life is more than meat and drink and fun and fortune. However, it is often easy for young people to follow the line of least resistance and to be found to be "even as chaff is driven before the wind, or as a vessel is tossed about upon the waves, without sail or anchor, or without anything wherewith to steer her" (Mormon 5:18).

Paul indicated that we all could attain this abundant life by perfecting ourselves. The fact that most of us are far from perfection is not to say we cannot reach perfection, but we don't. Christ became perfect. He overcame. He suffered hunger, thirst, cold, heat, pain, sorrow, and all that life has to offer in suffering. Each time he overcame, he became more nearly perfect. Paul said:

"And being made perfect, he became the author of eternal salvation unto all them that obey him" (Hebrews 5:9).

"For it became him, for whom are all things, and by whom are all things, in bringing many sons unto glory, to make the captain of their salvation perfect through sufferings" (Hebrews 2:10).

Perfection is a long, hard journey with many pitfalls. It's not attainable overnight. Eternal vigilance is the price of victory. Eternal vigilance is required in the subduing of enemies and in becoming the master of our lives. It cannot be accomplished in little spurts and disconnected efforts. There must be constant and valiant, purposeful living—righteous living.

Do we have the power to attain this kind of abundance? The psalmist was inspired to write:

"What is man, that thou art mindful of him? and the son of man, that thou visitest him?

"For thou hast made him a little lower than the angels, and hast crowned him with glory and honour.

"Thou madest him to have dominion over the works of thy hands; thou hast put all things under his feet" (Psalm 8:4–6).

There are those today who say that man is the result of his environment and cannot rise above it. Those who justify mediocrity, failure, immorality of all kinds, and even weakness and criminality are certainly misguided. Surely the environmental conditions found in childhood and youth are an influence of power. But the fact remains that every normal soul has its free agency and the power to row against the current and to lift itself to new planes of activity and thought and development. Man can transform himself. Man must transform himself.

Abraham did. He came out of an idol-worshiping family; yet he headed a dispensation of worshipers of the true and living God. Moses was born to poverty and slavery, was reared in luxury and court honors, and had great opportunities. He rose to the heights which man can attain and walked and talked with God. Saul of Tarsus was born and reared and trained, but he completely transformed himself and became an apostle of the Lord. Saul, the king of Israel, came of humble birth—even the Lord did—but when Samuel had dealt with him and anointed him and trained him, he became another person. God gave him another heart and turned him into another man.

Arnold Bennett is quoted as saying: "The real tragedy is the tragedy of a man who never in his life braces himself for his one supreme effort, who never stretches to his full capacity, never stands up to his full stature. To lie down and moan and whine about limited opportunities is the part of weaklings. To grasp the opportunities at hand and walk forward is the way of the strong."

To the Corinthians Paul said this: "And every man that striveth for the mastery is temperate in all things. Now they do it to obtain a corruptible crown; but we an incorruptible" (1 Corinthians 9:25).

Self-mastery, then, is the key, and every person should study his own life, his own desires and wants and cravings, and bring them under control.

Man can transform himself and he must. Man has in himself the seeds of godhood, which can germinate and grow and develop. As the acorn becomes the oak, the mortal man becomes a god. It is within his power to lift himself by his very bootstraps from the plane on which he finds himself to the plane on which he should be. It may be a long, hard lift with many obstacles, but it is a real possibility.

In other words, environment need not be our limit. Circumstance may not need to be our ruler, nor do granite walls or walls of steel need to be our prison.

To be perfect, one can turn to many areas as a starting place. (Converts join often in midlife and old age.) He or she must become the perfect husband, the perfect wife, the perfect father, the perfect mother, the perfect leader, and the perfect follower. One's marriage must be perfectly performed and perfectly kept on a hallowed plane. One must keep his life circumspect. Each person must keep himself clean and free from lusts, from adultery and homosexuality, and from drugs. He must shun ugly, polluted thoughts and acts as he would an enemy. Pornographic and erotic stories and pictures are worse than polluted food. Shun them. The body has power to rid itself of sickening food. The person who entertains filthy stories or pornographic pictures and literature records them in his marvelous human computer, the brain, which can't forget such filth. Once recorded, it will always remain there, subject to recall.

As we have stated before, the way to perfection seems to be a changing of one's life—to substitute the good for the evil in every case. Changes can come best if we take one item at a time.

The more we are guided by eternal considerations in our conduct, the better we will manage mortality. The more we understand Jesus' teachings concerning the purpose of life, the greater will be our sense of belonging and our sense of identity. The more we come to accept the Fatherhood of God, the better able we will be to implement the brotherhood of man. The more we understand what really happened in the life of Jesus of Nazareth in Gethsemane and on Calvary, the better able we will be to understand the importance of sacrifice and selflessness in our lives.

We live in a world in which there is increasing selfishness and increasing assertiveness on the part of many who make more and more demands of others and fewer and fewer demands of themselves.

Selfishness at either end of its journey makes of an individual a bundle of appetites. Such individuals neither have distinctive personalities nor are they interesting to know. But the person who lives the abundant life is the person we find ourselves wanting to be around, wanting to talk to, wanting to learn from. In this world, such individuals will be at a premium and will attract to them thoughtful and wise friends who want to partake of their influence.

Finally, the abundant life does not simply

consist of living longer or more years. It is a matter of height and attainment rather than the mere length of life itself. Thanks to Jesus of Nazareth and his atonement, we will all receive the gift of immortality—endless individual existence—but only if we follow his teachings will we be able to live abundantly in this world and even more abundantly in the world to come.

From an address given at Weber State College on 4 November 1977, while President Kimball was serving as president of The Church of Jesus Christ of Latter-day Saints (see *Ensign*, July 1978, 3–7).